PATTY!

THE SPORTS CAREER OF PATRICIA BERG

BY:

JAMES & LYNN HAHN

EDITED BY:

DR. HOWARD SCHROEDER

Professor in Reading and Language Arts
Dept. of Elementary Education
Mankato State University

CRESTWOOD HOUSE

Mankato, Minnesota

CIP

LIBRARY OF CONGRESS CATALOGING IN PUBLICATION DATA

Hahn, James.
  Patty! The sports career of Patricia Berg.

  (Sports legends)
  SUMMARY: Presents a biography of the first person honored in World
Golf Hall of Fame.
  1. Berg, Patricia Jane, 1918-   — Juvenile literature. 2. Golfers —
United States — Biography — Juvenile literature. [1. Berg, Patricia Jane,
1918-   . 2. Golfers] I. Hahn, Lynn, joint author. II. Schroeder, Howard.
III. Title. IV. Series.
GV964.B47H33   796.352'902'4   [B]   [92]   80-28744
ISBN 0-89686-127-9 (lib. bdg.)
ISBN 0-89686-142-2 (pbk.)

INTERNATIONAL STANDARD BOOK NUMBERS: 0-89686-127-9 Library Bound 0-89686-142-2 Paperback	**LIBRARY OF CONGRESS CATALOG CARD NUMBER:** 80-28744

PHOTO CREDITS:

Cover: Wilson Sporting Goods Company

Wilson Sporting Goods Co.: 3, 5, 10, 18-19, 31, 32-33,
      39, 41, 43, 46
UPI: 8, 15, 16, 21, 25, 26, 29, 35, 37, 38, 44-45
U.S. Golf Association: 13
Wide World Photos: 22, 28

CRESTWOOD HOUSE

Crestwood House, Inc., Box 3427, Hwy. 66 So., Mankato, MN 56001

PATTY!

CHAPTER 1

Patty Berg is one of the greatest golf legends of all time. During the 1930's, '40's, '50's, '60's, '70's, and '80's, she won over eighty golf tournaments both as an amateur and a professional. Patty won her first golf tournament when she was sixteen years old and her last at forty-four. Reporters voted her Woman Athlete of the Year at three different times, 1938, 1943, and 1955. Patty Berg was one of the original thirteen golfers enshrined in the World Golf Hall of Fame.

The road to the top of the golf world was interesting for Patty. Patricia Jane Berg was born on February 13, 1918 in Minneapolis, Minnesota. Patty's background was Irish and Norwegian. Her mother's name was Therese and her father's was Herman. Mr. Berg owned a grain company and sold and traded on the Minneapolis Grain Exchange.

Patty went to John Burroughs Grammar School. Golf didn't interest her at that time. Football and baseball took up most of her free time. She liked track too, and set a grammar school track record in 1930. She also played hockey. Whenever she had the puck, she was a scoring threat.

But her main love was football. When she grew

4

up, she wanted to be a football player.

On a vacant lot near her home, Patty played football with some boys. All the boys wanted her on their team because she was a good quarterback. She passed, tackled, and kicked as well as any boy her age. She could take the hard bumps and tackles too. Although Patty was chubby, everyone liked her. She always had a cheerful smile.

Most of the time Patty played football for a team called the "50th Street Tigers." They had only one play. Patty would yell, "22," and everyone

Patty shows the form that made her famous.

would run whichever way they wanted. The Tigers didn't lose any games. Bud Wilkinson, one of the "Tigers," later coached football at the University of Oklahoma and for the St. Louis Cardinals in the National Football League.

One afternoon after school, Patty's football career suddenly ended. She had just played a rough game with her brother, Herman, Jr., and some other boys. Patty's knees were bruised and her face scratched. She hadn't changed her clothes after school and her new dress was ripped. The pretty collar was torn and she couldn't even find the belt.

Running home as fast as she could, Patty wanted to fix the dress before her mother saw it. All the sewing machines in the world, her brother told her, could never fix that dress.

When Patty's mother saw what was left of the dress, she was very upset. She marched Patty in to see her father. Patty's mother told him she had bought the dress only yesterday. It wasn't even paid for yet! Her parents decided Patty shouldn't play football anymore, so she stood on the sidelines and watched.

Speed skating interested Patty next. She joined a famous speed-skating club, the Powder Horn Club, in Minneapolis. She won some trophies and skated in the national tournament. There Patty finished third in the nation in the Junior Class. She later quit ice skating because she says she "lost too many races by a nose," and felt she wasn't good enough.

CHAPTER 2

Patty's father enjoyed golf and interested her in the game. After school at Ramsey Junior High School, she liked swinging her dad's golf clubs in the back yard.

When Patty was thirteen, her father bought her brother a membership at a golf club. Patty asked why she couldn't have one, too. Just because she was a girl, she said, was no reason not to buy her a membership. Her dad agreed and bought one for Patty. But, he told her it cost a lot of money so she had to golf every day to make it worthwhile.

Since Patty didn't have her own golf clubs, her dad gave her four of his old ones. He cut down a brassie (two-wood) so she could use it. Since she didn't know anything about golf, her dad taught her how to grip the club and swing. A careful, patient teacher, he showed his daughter how the best golfers in the world hit the ball. His hobby was taking movies of famous golfers and studying their swings. He told Patty she could be a good golfer if she practiced and studied golf. They spent many happy hours together practicing and playing golf.

At first, Patty's golf was awful. The first day on the golf course she lost six golf balls. Once she drove the ball into a rock and the ball bounced back almost hitting her. It took her a long time to learn to play well. At one point, Patty's father arranged for instruction from professional golfers, Willie Kidd and Jim Pringle, from Interlachen Country Club to help improve her game.

Patty hit the ball into the rough and sand traps many times. Once, when in a sand trap, she swung

Patty blasts out of trouble in a 1953 tournament.

at the ball wildly. She hit a line drive and almost hit a golfer thirty yards away. But, after many hours of practice, she became a super sand player. Some golfers said she was probably the best in the world. With a smile, Patty said she had to be a great sand player, since she spent more time in sand traps than anybody else.

In 1933, at age fifteen, she entered her first golf tournament, the Minneapolis City Championship.

In the first round, Patty shot 122, a very poor score. In the match play part of the tournament, she lost almost every hole. Her first tournament was a failure. But, she learned a major lesson that day. She said she would try never to play so poorly again. Patty hoped to do much better in the next Minneapolis City Championship. She made plans to practice and train every day of the year.

The next morning Patty got up early to start practicing. Then, she practiced at least one hour every day. If she played poorly, she practiced more. In March, Patty wore a snowsuit and hit golf ball after golf ball. She stared at the ball and gritted her teeth. Then she swung, leaning into the ball for distance.

Patty also worked on the mental part of her game. She gained the will to win, courage, and a never-give-up attitude. Determination was Patty's motto. She firmly believed in a quote from Gary Player's book — "you must want to win, believe you will win, and think only winning thoughts." Patty aimed for perfection and never forgot the mistakes she made in 1933.

In the 1934 Minneapolis City Tournament, Patty cut forty strokes off her 1933 qualifying score. All her work paid off when she won the match play

Patty poses with the tools of her trade.

title. As a reward, her dad bought her new golf clubs: ten irons and five woods. She appreciated the irons and woods so much she took them into her bedroom and lined them against the wall before going to sleep.

Patty spent most of the summer of 1934 golfing. While at a summer camp in northern Minnesota, she got homesick for her golf course in Minneapolis and could hardly wait to get back home.

The seventeen-year-old won her first important tournament, the Minnesota State Championship, in 1935. A newspaper said she played with a "determination that if she loses, she will have to be beaten by her own opponent, because Miss Patty is not going to beat herself."

Because Patty was only seventeen years old she sometimes would feel a bit nervous playing with some of the finest golfers in the country. Once that summer Patty was playing in an exhibition match with golf pros Walter Hagen, John Revolta, and Horton Smith. More people followed them around the golf course than Patty had ever seen.

Patty was so tense she couldn't hit the ball straight. She kept hitting into the rough. On the first nine holes, she hit five people in the crowd. Later, Patty told reporters she looked at her freckles and was so scared they seemed to be popping out.

After shooting a 105, Patty was discouraged. But, her mother's reassurance convinced her to play again. After practicing many hours at the Northland Golf Club in Duluth, Minnesota, Patty became more confident of herself and her game.

Nervousness didn't upset Patty very much later that summer. She golfed into the finals of the most important tournament for women at that time, the United States National Amateur Championship. In one match, she beat Mrs. Dan Chandler. Amazing her fans with 200-yard drives, Patty won five matches in a row. But, after seventeen holes of a semi-final match, she was one down to Charlotte Glutting. On the eighteenth green, Patty sank a forty-five foot putt to tie the match. Then she won the match on the third extra hole.

In the final match, Patty played Glenna Collett Vare. Glenna had won the National Championship five times before. That afternoon, seven thousand fans followed Patty and Glenna around Interlachen Country Club in Minneapolis. Wearing a sweat shirt, the freckle-faced, red-haired Patty played well. Many fans felt the match was over when Glenna was four holes ahead with six holes left to play. Then Patty won the next three holes. However, Glenna birdied the 34th hole to win the match three and two.

Although only seventeen, Patty had placed second in the most important golf tournament in the United States. After the tournament, Patty and her father celebrated with ice cream cone treats.

Wearing the sweat shirt that she played in, Patty poses with the trophy she was trying to win. She had to settle for second in the 1935 National Championship.

13

CHAPTER 3

At seventeen, Patty weighed 115 pounds and stood five feet one inch tall. Although short, she hit long drives. Patty spent many hours practicing to improve all parts of her game. She spent as much time practicing as she did playing.

Patty's putting stroke was the best part of her game. Many fans said she stroked her putter as well as one of the finest golfers at the time, Bobby Jones. Helen Hicks, a great woman golfer, said Patty expected to hole every putt. When she missed one, she practiced until the turf cried out for mercy. After Patty missed a putt, she'd cry out, "Patricia!"

In 1936, Patty putted into the winner's cup five times. She won five of the twelve tournaments she entered. Many times she struggled to win after poor starts. Her fans included men who were amazed at the strength of her shots and women who adored her.

That year, Patty wore the same skirt she had worn in the 1935 national tournament. The skirt was too long and straight for 1936 styles, but she thought it brought good luck.

For her fine play in 1935 and 1936, the United States Golf Association (USGA) elected Patty to the

Reversing the outcome of their 1935 match, Patty beat Glenna Vare to win the 1936 Palm Beach Championship.

Curtis Cup team. The Curtis Cup team is top American women golfers who play a team of British women golfers. In 1936, the Curtis Cup matches were held in Scotland. Patty had a tough time, losing several matches. Some reporters wrote she was a little nervous and shouldn't have been on the

Fans in Minneapolis gave Patty flowers at a reception in her honor, following her good tournament play in 1936.

team.

After she returned home, Patty's father suggested she quit golf if it was making her nervous. She said she wasn't that nervous. Realizing how much she wanted to play, her father let her continue.

Staying in great shape was one reason Patty won so many tournaments in 1936 and throughout her career. She didn't smoke or drink alcoholic beverages. During tournaments, she ate only breakfast and dinner. For breakfast she had eggs and bacon with toast and jam or honey. Sometimes she would have only skim milk with cereal and toast. At dinner she had chicken or meat, with a salad, vegetable, and a cup of soup. She didn't eat many starchy foods. During tournaments, she went to bed early.

Attitude is another reason Patty won so often. When she didn't win she wasn't a poor sport. After losing, she bowed her head for a moment and blinked back tears. Then she'd lift her head and square her shoulders. She'd tell reporters her mistakes and praise the winner. After a loss, she didn't second-guess and make excuses. Usually, she said, "I did the best I could."

After learning more about pressure, nervousness didn't bother Patty as much. Before a tournament she'd tell reporters, "I'm going to play the very best I can. If I win — fine! If I don't win, I will next

Patty sizes up a putt.

time when it's my turn. Everyone has a turn. You can't expect to win always. But I believe if you do your very best, victory will come."

A cool, businesslike golfer, Patty rarely got ruffled and seldom let one poor shot upset her. Her dad used to say, "This shows her guts!" She carefully thought out the result of each shot before swinging.

When she wasn't golfing, Patty enjoyed shopping. She liked pretty, tailored clothes, but not fancy clothes. She wanted her dance dresses fashioned on sports lines and wore very little make-up. She especially liked shoes, although Patty didn't like shoes with very high heels. She liked all colors, but her favorite was navy blue.

Music also pleased Patty. One of her favorite songs was "Alone," sung by Kitty Carlisle and Allan Jones. The tango was a popular dance during the 1930's but Patty liked the waltz best. She enjoyed rhythm and loved to dance.

At nineteen, Patty said her ambition was, "to make the very best out of life that I can."

Patty made the best out of life in 1937, winning four tournaments. But she lost to Estelle Lawson Pate in the finals of the U.S. Amateur. Patty was so jittery, reporters said, she could hardly hold a club. Reporters felt that she lost because she was too young and inexperienced. Still, at nineteen, she was runner-up in the most important tournament for the second time.

Patty practiced more, and in 1938 golfed her way into the record books. She entered thirteen tournaments and won ten. That year she won the United States National Women's Amateur.

The 1938 National Amateur was at Westmore-

Patty shot a 308 to win the 1938 Women's Western Open. The score was an all-time women's record for 72 holes.

Patty finally won the Women's National Championship in 1938. She beat defending champion, Estelle Page, to win her first national title.

land Country Club in Wilmette, Illinois. In the final match, Patty played Estelle Page, who had beaten her in the 1937 finals.

In the afternoon round, Patty putted great. She had seven one-putt greens in thirteen holes. On the 31st green, she won the title, six and five. After Patty won, Estelle Page plopped a kiss on her cheek. The gallery of three thousand yelled themselves hoarse. Reporters said Patty played "as though she had her ball hypnotized."

Since she played so well, the Associated Press voted Patty Woman Athlete of the Year in 1938.

In the fall of 1938, Patty entered the University of Minnesota to take business courses. She practiced golf in the afternoons and studied at night. Sometimes she missed school to play in tournaments. But she still studied. One quarter she earned three B's and one C. She was one of the football team's best fans. Reading the sports pages each day, she quoted the baseball players' batting and fielding averages. She played softball with a women's team, and frequently hit home runs.

With blue eyes, curly, red hair, and hundreds of freckles, Patty was popular. But, she said she hated freckles and spent more money on freckle cream than anything else. Still, many boys asked her for dates. Most of the boys were athletes.

CHAPTER 4

Thanks to many hours of practice, Patty had a super start in 1939. She won six tournaments. Since she had the will to do well, Patty played well. She said she spent many hours practicing and studying her swing. She was eager to practice. To her, practicing was as much fun as playing.

On the practice tee, Patty developed grace, timing, and rhythm. She didn't gain these qualities in a few months. It took years of practice and hard work. She told reporters there was no short cut to success in golf. The only path to the top was by the practice tee. At practice, she was just as careful with her swing as during a tournament.

Although she was serious about golf, the fans loved Patty. She had a pleasant grin for the crowd and never became angry. After hitting a bad shot, she'd yell, "Patricia!" She never used nasty language.

Despite her wins, 1939 wasn't lucky for Patty. A month before her National Amateur crown, she had her appendix removed. She couldn't play in the tournament and lost by default. Then, on Christmas Day, Patty's mother died.

Patty wanted to quit golf. After a few weeks,

she decided her mother wouldn't have liked that. Although still grieving for her mother, Patty golfed in 1940. But she didn't play as well as she had before. She won only the Helen Lee Doherty Tournament and the Mid-Florida Championship.

Later in 1940, Patty decided to be a professional golfer. As an amateur, she had already won over forty tournaments. She signed a contract with the Wilson Sporting Goods Company and joined their advisory staff. Part of her job was to give golf clinics and exhibitions. Wilson Sporting Goods sold "Patty Berg" golf clubs, which are still available today.

When she wasn't giving clinics and exhibitions, Patty entered the few tournaments open to women pros. There were only three golf tournaments open

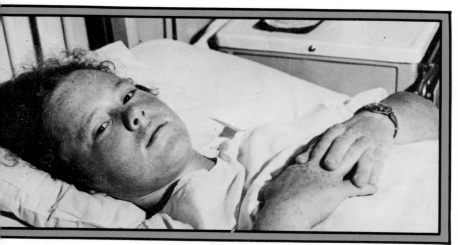

Patty recovers after her appendix was removed at a Minneapolis hospital.

to women pros at that time. The total prize money was about $500.

1941 was a big year for Patty. She won her first tournament as a pro, the Women's Western Open. Her prize was a $100 war bond. The twenty-three-year-old also won the Ashville Open and the Lake Champlain Invitational Open.

December, 1941, started out to be a happy month. Patty's father married Vera Parks on December 6. Patty had introduced them to each other while playing in an exhibition. She and Vera were to become close friends.

Patty talks to another great golfer, Sam Snead, at a 1939 tournament.

But on December 8, 1941, Patty's life changed. She had just finished golfing in Texas and was driving to Memphis, Tenn. to help raise money for the British War Relief. Suddenly, a car sped out of a side road and crashed into the car Patty was riding in.

Patty was thrown into the windshield, the glass cutting her face. Her left knee was broken in three places and torn open. Later, she told reporters her first thought was she'd never golf again.

Patty was in the hospital for a month, and rested at home for many more months. When the doctors took her leg out of the cast, they discovered that adhesions had formed. She was unable to bend her knee properly.

Patty had to work to get her knee in shape. She spent six months in Mobile, Alabama, exercising and training. Each day she bicycled, and worked out in a gym. She even punched a punching bag to get her timing back.

Hitting hundreds of golf balls daily, Patty worked to regain her skills. Les Bolstad, a golf pro in Minneapolis and one of Patty's coaches for many years helped Patty build and improve her swing.

In July, 1943, Patty made her comeback to tournament golf. She entered the Women's Western Open at Glen Oak Country Club near Chicago, Illinois. Shooting a 76, she amazed her fans and won the qualifying medal. Then, she won four matches in a row.

A happy Patty accepts the trophy for winning the 1943 Women's Western Open.

In the final match, Patty was three down to Dorothy Kirby on the 31st hole. Before teeing off that morning, Patty said she would never give up. She won the next four holes and pulled ahead with a birdie on the 35th hole to win the tournament.

It took Patty many months to regain her skills. She won only one more tournament that year, the All American Open at Tam O'Shanter in Niles, Illinois. But, honoring her comeback, reporters voted her Woman Athlete of the Year for the second time.

In September, after the All American Open, Patty joined the Marine Corps Women's Reserve and went to Officers' Training School. Early in the morning, or on a day of leave, Patty still practiced golf. She and Johnny Revolta won the Pro-Lady National Tournament in 1944. In 1945, Patty received an honorable discharge from the Marines. Her rank was first lieutenant.

After getting out of the Marines, it didn't take Patty long to get in shape. In 1946, she won four tournaments, including the Women's National Open.

That year's United States Women's Open was the first national open championship for women. They played at the Spokane Country Club in Washington. Winning the qualifying medal, Patty shot 73,

Patty is sworn into the Marine Corps Reserve in 1943.

72. Then in the final she beat Betty Jameson of San Antonio, Texas, 5 and 4. Patty won $5,600 in war bonds.

Patty was one of the most popular golfers at that time. Fans cheered her golf shots everywhere she played. Many wanted to shake her hand. "Good heavens," she squeaked when excited. But, during interviews, she blushed.

CHAPTER 5

In 1947, Patty had another good year. She won the Northern California Women's Open, the Pebble Beach Open, and the Northern California Medal Play Tournament. However, not all her time was spent in golf matches. She toured the country, visited schools, and talked to young people about golf. She gave clinics, exhibitions, encouragement, and laughs. She'd ask them, "You've heard Mark Twain's definition of golf, haven't you?" When no one answered, she'd say, "He called it a nice walk ruined."

In January 1948, Patty made golf history. She, Babe Zaharias, Babe's husband, George and Fred Corcoran, the first tournament director, had a meeting in Miami, Florida. They reorganized the profes-

Here's the young champion on her way to another victory.

sional golf tour for women. They named their group the Ladies' Professional Golfers Association (LPGA). Patty was elected its first president. She held that title for four years.

Office work didn't hurt Patty's golf. In 1948 she

won the Titleholders tournament, the Women's Western Open and the Hardscrabble Open.

The winner's check was signed by Patty Berg three times in 1949. At thirty-one, she won the Tampa Open, the Texas PGA Championship, and the Hardscrabble Open. For her outstanding play,

Babe Zaharias (right) and Patty started the Ladies Professional Golfer's Association in 1948.

the *Los Angeles Times* voted her Woman Golfer of the Year.

In 1950 Patty won the Hardscrabble Open for the third year in a row. She also won three other tournaments.

During the Weathervane tournament in 1951,

Patty beat Babe Zaharias in a 36-hole play-off. Babe shot 147, Patty 146. Patty became captain of the Weathervane International team by winning that tournament. The international team played a team of British women golfers and British men golfers. That year Patty also won the Sandhills Open and the Women's Western Open. She also was elected to the LPGA Hall of Fame.

On April 26, 1952, Patty set two world records for women. She shot 30 for nine holes and 64 for eighteen holes during the Richmond Open in Richmond, California. Those records stood for twelve years. Patty won the Richmond Open, plus two others that year.

Excellent is the only word to describe Patty's golf in 1953. She won five tournaments outright and tied for first in the Phoenix Weathervane Open. Patty also won the Vare Trophy. The trophy, named after Glenna Collett Vare, is awarded each year to the woman shooting the lowest average score. That year Patty had a 75.00 scoring average.

Jim Murray, a reporter, said Patty was "probably the greatest fairway wood player, man or woman, or boy, ever to pull a spoon (three-wood) out of a bag and rifle it to a pin."

Patty is shown on the way to her record-setting round at the Richmond Open in 1952.

CHAPTER 6

At age thirty-six, Patty won three women's tournaments. With Pete Cooper, she also won the Orlando Mixed Two-Ball tournament. That year she won the most money on the LPGA tour, $16,011.

In 1955, Patty won five tournaments and was named Woman Athlete of the Year for the third time. Her 74.47 scoring average won the Vare Trophy for the second time. Once again she topped the money list earning $16,492.

Patty won only the Dallas Open and Arkansas Open in 1956. But she won the Vare Trophy for the third time with a 74.57 scoring average.

Patty didn't like winning only two tournaments, so she practiced more. Her work paid off in 1957 when she won the Havana Open, the Augusta Titleholders, the Women's Western Open, and the World Championship. Her $16,272 in prize money led all the women pros.

Celebrating her fortieth year of life, Patty won the 1958 Women's Western Open and the American Open. Finally, age was catching up with her. She didn't win any tournaments in 1959 but won the American Open in 1960.

Not even "body English" would make this putt fall in the hole, and Patty lost the 1956 Serbin Women's Tourney by one stroke.

The master of the sand trap shows how it's done during a 1957 tournament.

Patty won the 1957 Augusta Titleholders Tournament.

Patty Berg won her last tournament, the Muskogee Open, in 1962. She accomplished what few athletes have — at forty-four years of age, Patty was still winning.

Slow down? Take it easy? Not Patty Berg. She just added more golf events to her schedule. She put on more golf clinics and exhibitions than anyone in the history of golf. In 1962, she became the first American woman golfer to put on clinics in Japan. She flew there, but told reporters she didn't like flying. Patty was tense on airplanes. Every time she saw the engines reverse on prop planes, she thought they were going to fall off.

When Patty returned to San Francisco from Japan, she was told the sad news that her father had suffered a stroke, from which he did not recover.

In 1963, Patty spent two months touring Europe. She told people, "watch your grips, check your stance, and bring the club straight back smooth and steady." She put on clinics and exhibitions in the Netherlands, Sweden, Scotland, Switzerland, Belgium, England, France, and Germany.

Traveling so much, Patty said, was one reason she never married. On the road ten or eleven months every year, she never stayed in one place very long.

Although no longer winning tournaments, Patty was still honored. In 1963, she won the Bobby Jones Sportsmanship Award. The USGA gives this prize

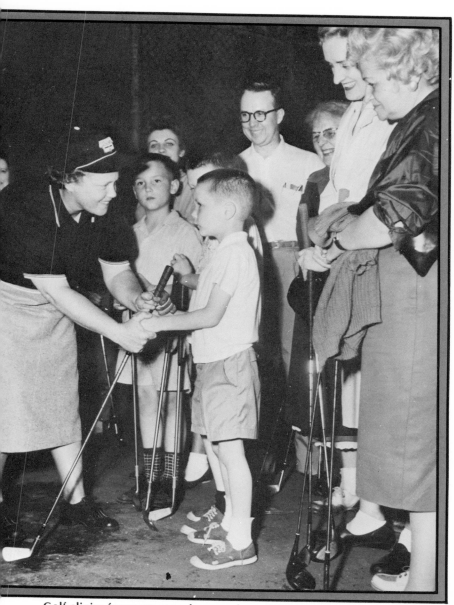

Golf clinics for young people were always important to Patty.

each year for sportsmanship. In 1969, Patty was honored with a golf tournament, The Patty. Berg Golf Classic.

CHAPTER 7

In February, 1971, Patty fought through her hardest round. She was stricken with cancer. After surgery, she spent many days in the hospital. Then, helped by three nurses, she struggled through a tough training program. Patty returned to Tommy Littleton's gym in Mobile, Alabama where she had trained after her knee surgery. Exercising each day, she was well enough by the end of 1971 to put on some golf clinics and exhibitions. "This time," she told reporters, "wasn't like when I broke my knee. I've worked just as hard. But I never got all my energy back. The cancer surgery took a very big toll."

Golfers around the world knew Patty was an all-time great. In 1972, she was elected to the American Golf Hall of Fame. The World Golf Hall of Fame voted Patty a member in 1974. At the ceremony, the audience laughed when she said, "I'm very happy I gave up football or I wouldn't be here tonight."

In 1975, the St. Paul, Minnesota Jaycees renamed their ladies' tournament the Patty Berg Classic. At that time, Patty's curly red hair was speckled with white and she wore glasses.

At age fifty-nine, Patty still kept a record of every golf shot she hit. The reason, she said, was to be true and fair to herself. It didn't matter if it was a tournament, a clinic, or exhibition. At home, she checked her record book. She wanted to see where her golf wasn't as good as it should have been. If she hit bad three-irons, she'd practice them. If it was driving, she'd practice that.

When not on the golf course, Patty wrote her third book on golf lessons.

Patty Berg gave nearly fifty years of her life to golf. She overcame sickness and tragedy to become one of the greatest golf legends.

Patty poses with trophies for the tournament named in her honor.

Patty and veteran men's pro, Gene Sarazen, teamed up in the 1976 Pepsi-Cola Mixed Team Championship.

AFTERWORD

Patty is currently living in Florida. On May 28, 1980 Patty had hip surgery in Minneapolis, Minnesota. She once again had to do strenuous exercises and training to regain her strength. She exer-

cises every day by hitting golf balls, swimming and bicycling. She continues to work for Wilsons Sporting Goods giving clinics and exhibitions, (she's now given well over ten thousand) and would still like to play in tournaments. Patty was Cancer Crusade Chairman for the state of Florida in 1979 and 1980.

PATTY BERG ACHIEVEMENTS

1936 - Member, Curtis Cup Team

1938 - Member, Curtis Cup Team
  Voted Outstanding Woman Athlete of the Year, Associated Press
  Made Honorary Life Member Interlachen Country Club, Minneapolis, MN

1940 - Turned Professional. Joined Wilson's Advisory Staff

1943 - Voted Outstanding Woman Athlete of the Year, Associated Press.
  Enlisted in Marine Corps Women's Reserve.

1945 - Received Honorable Discharge Marine Corps Women's Reserve, Rank 1st Lt.

1948 - Co-Founder of the Ladies Professional Golf Association. Elected first President of
  LPGA (served as President four years).

1949 - Voted Woman Golfer of the Year, Los Angeles Times

1951 - Set World Record for par 72 golf course - 9 holes, 30; 18 holes, 64.
  Elected Ladies PGA Golf Hall of Fame.
  Captain, Weathervane International Team

1953 - Winner, Vare Trophy, 75 scoring average.

1954 - LPGA Leading Money Winner
  Elected Helms Foundation Hall of Fame

1955 - LPGA Leading Money Winner
  Winner Vare Trophy - 74.47 Scoring Average
  Voted Woman Athlete of the Year, Associated Press
  Voted Woman Golfer of the Year, Los Angeles Times
  Winner Serbin Diamond Golf Ball, 47 points
  Winner, Golf Digest Performance Average Award - .894 average

1956 - Winner, Vare Trophy, 74.57 scoring average
  Winner, Golf Digest Performance Average Award
  Winner, Babe Zaharias Memorial Trophy - .882 average
  Received The Kappa Kappa Gamma Fraternity Achievement Award

1957 - LPGA, Leading Money Winner
  Winner, Golf Digest Performance Average Award - .830 average

1958 - Received William Richardson Award
  First Woman Elected and inducted into the Minnesota Sports Hall of Fame
  Chairman, Clinic Committee, LPGA

1959 - Received Women's Golf Personality Award of the Year
  Co-Chairman, Clinic Committee, LPGA
  Scored Hole-in-One - 140 Yards, Churchill Valley Country Club, Pittsburgh, Pennsyl-
  vania. First hole-in-one ever scored in USGA Championship.

1960 - Chairman, Membership Committee, LPGA

1961 - Elected and inducted into the Florida Sports Hall of Fame
  Made Honorary Life Member - Lehigh Acres Country Club, Lehigh, Florida
  Made Honorary Life Member - Spencer Country Club, Spencer, Iowa

1962 - First Woman Professional Golfer to give exhibitions in Japan

1963 - Conducted clinics and exhibitions for two months throughout Great Britain and
  Europe.
  Received Bobby Jones Sportsmanship Award
  Received Boston Achievement Award

1966 - Honorary Chairman, 1966 USGA Women's Open Championship
  Made Honorary Life Member, Hazeltine National Golf Club, Chaska, Minnesota

1967 - Elected Charter Member, Class A - Ladies Professional Golf Association.

1969 - Made Honorary Life Member, St. Andrews Golf Club, West Chicago, Illinois.
  Held Patty Berg Golf Classic, Pleasant Valley Country Club, Sutton, Mass.

1970 - Selected to the first Ladies Professional Golfers Association All-American Shotmak-
  ing Team.

1972 - Elected and inducted into the American Golf Hall of Fame
Honored by Western Women's Golf Association and presented Western Medal.
1974 - Elected Charter Member and inducted into the World Golf Hall of Fame
Made Honorary Life Member, Cypress Lake Country Club, Fort Myers, Florida
Made Life Member, Lochmoor Country Club, Fort Myers, Florida
1975 - Received the Frank Leahy Golf Award
Elected and inducted into the Churchman's Sports Hall of Fame
University of Minnesota Women's Intercollegiate Fund renamed "The Patty Berg In-
tercollegiate Women's Fund," now called the "University of Minnesota Patty
Berg Development Fund."
Elected and inducted into the All-American Collegiate Golf Hall of Fame
Received Joe Graffis Award presented by National Golf Foundation
Received Ben Hogan Award
St. Paul Jaycees Ladies Golf Tournament renamed "Patty Berg Golf Classic."
Honored at Trans-National Amateur Championship, Oaks Country Club (formerly
Oakhurst Country Club), Tulsa, Oklahoma.
1976 - Received Humanitarian Sportsman's Award of the United Cerebral Palsy Association
of Westchester County, Inc. (first woman to receive this award), for her contin-
uing contributions to the game of golf and mankind.
1977 - First annual Patty Berg Southwest Florida Pro-Am held at the Cypress Lake Country
Club, Fort Myers, Florida, and sponsored by the Cypress Lake Women's Golf
Association and the Southwest Florida PGA.
Published third book, "Inside Golf for Women," by Patty Berg and Marsh Schiewe.
First Book, "Golf," by Patty Berg and Otis Dypwyck, published in 1941; sec-
ond book, "Golf Illustrated," by Patty Berg and Mark Cox, published in 1950.
1978 - The 1978 Women's South Atlantic Golf Championship (Sally Tournament) desig-
nated in honor of Patty Berg
Received Honorary Life Membership, Oceanside Country Club, Ormond Beach, FL.
Elected and inducted into the PGA Hall of Fame (second woman to be elected)
Honored on her 60th birthday by the Commissioner of the Ladies Professional Golf
Association, his staff and all members of the Ladies Professional Golf Associ-
ation and members of other affiliated golf organizations.
Elected Honorary Member of the LPGA Teaching Division.
Received the Gold Tee Award presented by the Metropolitan Golf Writers Assoc.
Dedication of the Patty Berg Room at Interlachen Country Club, Edina, Minnesota.
Honorary Chairperson of the Hubert H. Humphrey Celebrity Open.
Ladies Professional Golf Association established the Patty Berg Award.
Gift for Mt. Scopus Reborn, Israel, presented by the Philadelphia Chapter of
Hadassah in honor of Patty Berg.
1979 - American Cancer Society, Florida Division's Crusade Chairman.
Received the City of Hope Special Victor Award in conjunction with Sport's Illu-
strated's 25th Anniversary for her contributions to the World of Sports during the
past 25 years.
Honorary Co-Chairperson of the ERA Kansas City LPGA Classic.
1980 - American Cancer Society, Florida Division's Crusade Chairman.
The National PGA Jr. Girls Championship Trophy designated "The Patty Berg Trophy."
1980 marked Patty Berg's Fortieth Anniversary with Wilson Sporting Goods Co.
Selected as one of the 125 all-time greatest athletes by sportswriters and broad-
casters who participated in the Miller 125 Sports Poll.
Elected and inducted into The Womens Sports Hall of Fame - Womens Sports Foundation.
1981 - Proclaimed Honorary Member of The Military Order of the World Wars.
Received the Sword of Hope Award
Received the Herb Graffis Award

IF YOU ENJOYED THIS STORY, THERE ARE MORE LEGENDS TO READ ABOUT:

PELÉ! THE SPORTS CAREER OF EDSON DO NASCIMENTO

HENRY! THE SPORTS CAREER OF HENRY AARON

TARK! THE SPORTS CAREER OF FRANCIS TARKENTON

BROWN! THE SPORTS CAREER OF JAMES BROWN

PATTY! THE SPORTS CAREER OF PATRICIA BERG

THORPE! THE SPORTS CAREER OF JAMES THORPE

ZAHARIAS! THE SPORTS CAREER OF MILDRED ZAHARIAS

SAYERS! THE SPORTS CAREER OF GALE SAYERS

CASEY! THE SPORTS CAREER OF CHARLES STENGEL

KILLY! THE SPORTS CAREER OF JEAN-CLAUDE KILLY

CHRIS! THE SPORTS CAREER OF CHRIS EVERT LLOYD

BABE! THE SPORTS CAREER OF GEORGE RUTH

KING! THE SPORTS CAREER OF BILLIE JEAN KING

WILT! THE SPORTS CAREER OF WILTON CHAMBERLAIN

ALI! THE SPORTS CAREER OF MUHAMMAD ALI

DATE DUE

JAN. 1 8		
MAR. 1 1		
JAN 19		

Hahn, James & Lynn
AUTHOR
Patty!
TITLE

DATE DUE	BORROWER'S NAME
	Kyle Y.

DEM

92
PAT